INJURED IN AN ACCIDENT:

WHAT YOU NEED TO KNOW

A GUIDE TO INJURY AND ACCIDENT LAW IN PENNSYLVANIA

BY LAURENCE B. GREEN

SPEAKER MEDIA PRESS

Injured in an Accident: What You Need to Know

ISBN 978-1-935411-27-7

Printed in the USA

DISCLAIMER

CONTENTS

About the Author

Attorney Laurence B. Green was born in Pittsburgh, PA in 1942. After high school, he enlisted in the U.S. Army, where he served in both South Korea and Japan. Following his military career, he attended the University of Pittsburgh and graduated with his bachelor's degree in 1966. Upon graduation, Mr. Green went to work as a laborer in the open hearth furnace at the Homestead Works of U.S. Steel and was a member of the United Steel Workers of America. Thereafter, he attended the University Of Pittsburgh School Of Law where he received his Juris Doctor in 1971.

Mr. Green began his legal career as a staff attorney for Neighborhood Legal Services Association. He then left that position to open a private law office in Pittsburgh in the general practice of law, concentrating in Plaintiff's Personal Injury litigation. He is a founding partner of the law firm of Berger and Green, P.C., where he represents injured accident victims as a personal injury attorney. Mr. Green handles personal injury claims ranging from car accidents, dog bites, and defective products, to slip and fall accidents.

Mr. Green is a hands-on attorney who is not afraid to take on a complex case. Clients trust Mr. Green's extensive knowledge and experience in personal injury cases. He understands the difficulties individuals face after an accident and is sensitive to their needs. He urges anyone who has been injured in an accident to seek experienced representation so they can recover damages. He wants his clients to focus on their recovery throughout this process and to know that Berger and Green is making their case a top priority.

Mr. Green is licensed to practice in all Pennsylvania State and Federal Courts and in the Supreme Court of the United States. He is a member of the American Association for Justice (AAJ), the Pennsylvania Association for Justice (PAJ), the Western Pennsylvania Trial Lawyers Association (WPTLA), the Pennsylvania Bar Association (PBA), and the Allegheny County Bar Association (ACBA). He is also an Allegheny County Bar Foundation Patron Fellow.

Attorney Green is part of a distinguished group called the Million Dollar Advocates Forum. This is a small group of attorneys throughout the United States who have successfully obtained awards in the amount of one million dollars or more for their clients. Attorney Green has been named as a Pennsylvania Super Lawyer. These lawyers represent the top five percent of all lawyers in Pennsylvania in peer recognition and professional achievement.

Attorney Green is a distinguished personal injury attorney who is proud to serve accident victims throughout Pennsylvania. He works hard to make sure his clients are treated fairly and with respect. Clients appreciate his hard work, dedication, and compassion.

INTRODUCTION

Berger and Green, P.C. is a Social Security Disability and Personal Injury Law firm located in Pittsburgh, Pennsylvania. We have been successfully representing individuals for over 40 years. Our attorneys are driven, dedicated, and knowledgeable. They understand that living with a disability or an injury is difficult, so they work hard for their clients to alleviate the added stress and challenges these troubling times can bring. At Berger and Green, we offer free case evaluations by phone, email, or a visit to your home or the hospital. There is never a fee charged unless we are able to successfully win your claim.

Due to our extensive knowledge and experience, our attorneys have a proven record in injury and disability claims. Clients appreciate our hard work and dedication to their case. The client's best interest is always put first at Berger and Green.

Berger and Green has advocated on behalf of thousands of injured and disabled individuals for more than 40 years. Our areas of practice include:

Motor Vehicle Accidents: Berger and Green handles all motor vehicle accidents which include car, truck, pedestrian, bicycle, motorcycle, bus, and train accidents.

Personal Injury: Berger and Green is committed to representing individuals who have been injured due to someone else's negligence or carelessness. These types of cases include slip-and-fall accidents and other premises liability claims, work accidents, farm accidents, construction accidents, day care accidents, dog bite attacks, swimming pool accidents, aviation accidents, boating accidents, and other general negligence-based claims.

Workers' Compensation: When an individual suffers from a work-related injury or illness, Berger and Green can help clients pursue their full wage and medical benefits. This includes work accident injuries, industrial accident injuries, repetitive stress injuries, occupational illness, aggravation of a pre-existing condition, and other work-related injuries.

Product Liability: It is a manufacturer's responsibility to make sure their products are safe for consumers. A manufacturer may become liable for damages and injuries resulting from dangerous and defective products. If someone is injured due to these defective products, he or she may be able to pursue a products liability claim to obtain compensation for their injuries.

Medical Malpractice: If you were injured or lost a loved one due to the medical negligence of a doctor, nurse, or hospital, a medical malpractice claim may be pursued.

Social Security Disability: Berger and Green helps people who are seeking Social Security Disability Insurance (SSDI) benefits and Supplemental Security Income (SSI) benefits. They are experienced in filing applications, appeals, and attending all Social Security hearings.

Visit our website at www.bergerandgreen.com to learn more about our firm and the cases we handle.

PART ONE

Chapter One

Injured In An Accident

If you are reading this book it is likely you or someone you care about has been injured in an accident. The first thing an individual should do if he or she has been injured in an accident is to get appropriate medical attention. Next, we advise our clients to follow through with the recommendations of their attending physician in seeking subsequent follow-up care and in taking medication that is prescribed.

Whenever possible, the police should be summoned to the scene of the accident or injury. This begins the gathering of documentation that is important in a personal injury case. In circumstances where a serious injury has occurred, there is often not an opportunity for the injured party to gather information at the scene of an accident. However, if it is possible, one should get the contact information and insurance information of the driver or other at fault party.

When To Retain A Lawyer

At Berger and Green, we recommend that an injured individual retain an experienced personal injury law firm and an attorney at the earliest appropriate time so that an investigation can be performed and evidence can be secured and preserved.

Importance of Medical Treatment

The value of your case will be determined by your injuries and medical treatment. It is imperative to your claim that you are treated by a physician and that you follow his or her orders and recommendations for follow-up treatment. We suggest that our clients keep a calendar of all appointments. Keep track of the doctors, specialists, and hospitals you have visited. Make note of things that your physician tells you and record how you are feeling. Taking photographs of how you are healing can also benefit your case. At Berger and Green we want you to focus on getting better, which includes getting the appropriate medical care so that you may recover.

The Preservation of Evidence

If you have been injured in an accident, you want the maximum compensation for your injuries. As your attorney, we at Berger and Green immediately begin building your case. We gather the evidence that supports the circumstances of your injuries. No matter how your injury occurred, whether it was an auto accident, slip and fall, or dog bite, it is important to document as much information about the scene as possible. This includes gathering the contact information of all parties involved and that of any witnesses to the injury. When possible, take pictures at the scene of the accident or shortly thereafter, including the license plate of the other parties involved. Remember to take photographs of the damage to your vehicle, including the damage to the exterior, interior, and under the hood. If you are recovering in the hospital, we strongly encourage that you have a friend or relative take pictures or video of the accident scene.

Choosing The Right Attorney

It is important you choose an attorney who has experience in handling personal injury matters. Experienced lawyers in this area of the law are willing to provide representation in these cases on a contingency fee basis. This means that the lawyer is willing to invest their time and talent in providing representation and does not get paid unless the case has a favorable outcome. You should interview the lawyer and make sure that you feel comfortable that he or she has the experience and knowledge to handle your case and that you would like to work with him or her. We suggest that you ask your prospective lawyer these questions: *How long have you been in practice? Do you concentrate your practice in the area of plaintiff's personal injury law? Have you handled a case that is similar to mine?* You will be working with your lawyer during the pendency of your case, which can last well over a year. Make sure that you are comfortable working with this person and that you feel comfortable that they are knowledgeable and care about you and your case. You should have a clear understanding of what to expect once you have hired an attorney.

Choose A Lawyer With Experience

Berger and Green has over 40 years of experience in handling all types of serious personal injury matters including motor vehicle accidents, slip and falls, dog bites, and defective products involving both adults and children. Every case is unique and we use our years of experience to achieve the best possible results for our clients.

CHAPTER 2

WHY YOU NEED A LAWYER

We believe that you need a lawyer to handle your accident claim in order to obtain the best possible recovery in your case. Many people try to handle their accident claim themselves and they end up getting less money. In a personal injury claim, there may be multiple at-fault parties and sources of insurance. As your attorney it is our responsibility to determine all sources of coverage. This can be very difficult to do if you do not have experience in this area. Also, determining the value of your claim requires attention to many factors including your medical bills, future medical care, lost wages, and pain and suffering. It is not the responsibility of the insurance carrier to offer you a fair settlement.

Your own insurance carrier is responsible for paying medical expenses and lost wage reimbursement if you have purchased it. However, your insurance carrier does not assist you, the insured, in making a claim against a negligent individual and their insurance company. Insurance companies have lawyers looking out for their best interests and so should you.

Your Lawyer Will Talk To The Insurance Companies

We recommend that you have your lawyer talk to and contact your insurance carrier as well as the carriers of the at-fault parties. It is your lawyer's job to speak with the insurance company. It is in your best interest to have an attorney represent you. At Berger and Green we speak with insurance adjusters every day and we know how to navigate the claims process.

It is important to remember that the insurance company has only its best interest in mind. Insurance companies are focused on settling your claim quickly and for the least amount of money possible. This can mean that dealing with the insurance company yourself can actually hurt your case in the long run.

Protect Your Rights

Hiring a lawyer allows one to have his or her rights protected. Adult individuals involved in an accident in Pennsylvania have two years from the date of the accident within which to either settle the case or have a lawsuit filed on their behalf. For the sake of caution, we treat the day before the 2nd anniversary of the accident as the last day to settle or file suit. Beyond that date their claim is barred by the statute of limitations. Children on the other hand have until their 20th birthday in which to either have a lawsuit filed on their behalf or to have settled their case before their claim is barred by the statute of limitations.

One big mistake we often see is a person attempting to resolve his or her case and waiting until just before the two year anniversary to contact an attorney. It is often difficult and risky for an attorney to step in at this point. An attorney may not have enough time to research and properly identify all parties correctly and name them in a lawsuit. There may also be inadequate time to gather all documentation that we prefer to have in hand when filing suit. If the at-fault party is deceased or cannot be located the problems are even worse. In addition, when an insurance company is notified of a claim or representation long after the underlying event, they are more likely to deny your claim, defend it more aggressively, and remain skeptical about your case.

Your Financial Security

Law firms make sure that your bills are taken care of by contacting all healthcare providers and ensuring their statements are submitted to the appropriate first party benefit or healthcare provider so that they can be considered for payment. Further, there may be bills that are outstanding and need to be addressed with the insurance carrier of the negligent party including medical bills, out of pocket expenses, and pain and suffering claims.

Hiring a lawyer will allow you to focus on your recovery. In the aftermath of an accident there is a lot of paperwork involved in making claims to your own insurance carrier for first-party benefits, medical expense reimbursement, lost wage reimbursement and also in making claims to those responsible for your injuries and damages. All cases are prepared as if they are going to trial. Along the way we attempt to secure a settlement for our clients, but only if that settlement is fair, reasonable, and adequate.

Represent You In Court

Berger and Green provides representation at trial if we conclude that the offer of settlement received is not fair, reasonable, or adequate. In this instance we will make a recommendation that you reject a low settlement offer and to authorize us to file a lawsuit on your behalf. Ultimately, you have the final say as to whether or not you wish to accept a settlement or reject that settlement and permit us to file a lawsuit on your behalf.

Contingency Fees

Personal injury cases are most often handled on a contingent fee basis. This means that you will not be charged a fee for legal services unless you win your case. Personal injury attorneys invest their time and talent into making a recovery on your behalf. In today's climate, it is also necessary for your attorney to advance significant costs to investigate and document your case. If your personal injury attorney is unsuccessful you do not owe any money. If you win your case you will be charged a specific fee and costs that were outlined in your fee agreement when you agreed to representation by your attorney.

Berger and Green Fees

At Berger and Green, we charge a contingent fee in personal injury cases. This includes motor vehicle accident cases that reach a settlement without going to trial and cases that must be litigated. We also work on a contingency fee basis in non-motor vehicle accident cases such as slip and falls, dog bites, defective products and the like.

Berger and Green advances all costs in connection with the case. At the successful completion of a case, the advanced costs are reimbursed. Should there be no recovery, there is no obligation on the behalf of our clients to reimburse Berger and Green for the advanced costs.

Dangers Of Settling A Case Without Representation

You may have received an offer to settle your case from the insurance company. We strongly advise you against settling your case before speaking with an attorney. Remember, it is free to speak with an experienced personal injury lawyer at Berger and Green. You have nothing to lose by calling a lawyer for a free evaluation of your case. At Berger and Green we offer a free, no-obligation evaluation of your case. If we think that the insurance company is offering you a fair settlement we will let you know. However, it has been our experience that the insurance company will not make a fair settlement offer the first time.

The priority of the insurance adjuster is to secure your name on a release for the least possible amount of money. The at-fault party's insurance company has an obligation to investigate the case and will attempt to settle the matter within the confines of the policy limit to protect its policyholder. They do not represent the interests of the injured plaintiff nor are they obligated to safeguard those interests. The insurance carrier deals with cases like this on a full time basis every day. They will not and do not provide information to an injured party to explain sources of recovery, potential defendants, the value of the damage claim, and whether or not there are multiple sources of recovery such as underinsured motorist benefits.

Once you sign a release you have signed away and given up any right that you have to make any further claim arising from the event which caused your injuries. The best way to protect yourself and your rights is to consult with a knowledgeable and experienced personal injury lawyer who can advise you about all of the issues that arise in your case and allow you to concentrate on getting better. Your lawyer will focus on presenting your case in the best possible light in order to obtain an advantageous settlement, or if that is not possible, to provide representation at the trial level.

Chapter 3

Report The Accident To Your Insurer

If you are involved in an accident you should report the accident to your insurance carrier as soon as is possible. This is true whether or not you are at fault for the accident, are an injured victim in an accident, or if your car has been damaged. Though it is important to contact your insurance carrier soon after an accident, we do not recommend that you discuss who is at fault in the accident without first contacting an attorney. You should also not tell the carrier that you are not injured until sufficient time has passed to be sure a slow developing injury will not manifest itself. It is not uncommon for swelling and pain to occur in the days following a car accident. If you are not experiencing pain tell your insurer that you do not want to discuss injuries at this time.

You will need to provide your insurance carrier with basic facts about the accident including the time and date, the location of the accident, and the parties involved in the accident. Your insurance carrier will want to know if there were injuries and if the police were present at the scene. Your first call to your insurance carrier is to report the accident only, this is not the time to provide a detailed report of your injuries or to discuss if you may or may not be at fault or partially at fault for the accident. Please do not make the assumption that because you have paid a premium for many months or years to your insurance carrier that they have your best interests at heart.

When you contact your insurance carrier you are seeking your first-party benefits. This includes medical care and wage loss benefits. You will need to sign an application for these benefits from your insurance carrier. It is best that you retain an attorney to review the application for benefits before returning the documents to your insurance company.

The Negligent Parties Insurance Company

We strongly discourage speaking with the at-fault driver's insurance company. Never discuss the details of the accident with the at-fault driver's insurance company.

Do Not Give A Recorded Statement

Do not speak with any other insurance carrier besides your own. The other person's insurance carrier may wish to take a recorded statement and may ask you questions which could seriously compromise your ability to make a damage claim. In this instance, what you say can and will be used against you. You are not required to give a recorded statement to the insurance company. The insurance company does not have a right to a recorded statement. If your insurance carrier requests a recorded statement, tell them that you would like to decide if you need a lawyer first. You do not owe the insurance carrier any further explanation.

The answers that are given during a recorded statement are permanent. This means that if you misunderstood a question, gave an incomplete answer (to a long multi-part question) or were tricked, your claim will likely be adversely affected.

Chapter 4

Who You Are Making A Claim Against

Liability claims are presented to the insurance carrier of the at-fault party. If a lawsuit is filed, then the defendant is the at-fault party named in the complaint. The at-fault party is represented by an insurance company that is obligated to defend the insured by hiring a lawyer, paying the lawyer, and paying plaintiff's damages within the confines of the at-fault party's insurance coverage.

Plaintiff's lawyers look to make claims against solvent defendants. If the defendant does not have insurance, it is most often a useless act to satisfy an award or judgement against someone that does not have significant assets.

If you are a passenger in an accident and you were injured due to the negligence of the driver who happens to be your friend or a family member, you may be hesitant to contact a personal injury lawyer. You must remember that your friend purchased liability insurance in case they were in an accident and injured someone. When you make a claim you are seeking coverage under the driver's liability policy, his or her personal assets are only at risk if you get a judgement or verdict that exceeds his or her liability coverage and you choose to go after his or her property. This is seldom, if ever, done.

If the at-fault party does not have insurance or has insufficient insurance, you can make a claim against your own uninsured and underinsured motorists benefits coverage if purchased. Making a claim against your underinsured or uninsured motorists benefits will not cause your rates to increase or your insurer to drop your coverage.

PA Financial Responsibility Law

The insurance system in the Commonwealth of Pennsylvania is governed by the Pennsylvania Financial Responsibility Law and is often referred to as "no-fault." The Pennsylvania Financial Responsibility Law does not mean that there is no one at fault when an accident occurs. Under the Pennsylvania Financial Responsibility Law, individuals involved in motor vehicle accidents are entitled to medical benefits, lost wages, and property damage from their own source of insurance through either the policy that they have purchased or a policy that is maintained by a resident relative in the home. If the individual does not have insurance, the source of coverage is through the policy of the driver in whose car they are an occupant. If the individual is a pedestrian and they have no coverage, the individual can then seek coverage from any vehicle involved in the accident. The amount of coverage depends on what the policy holder has purchased. This is regardless of who is at fault.

Chapter 5

Understand Your Insurance Coverage

It is very important that our clients understand their insurance coverage and benefits. In Pennsylvania, first-party benefits consist of medical reimbursement in a minimum amount of $5,000.00. This is the minimum amount of benefit required by law. Greater first-party medical benefits can be purchased and are recommended.

First Party Medical Benefits

First party benefits include not only hospital and doctor visits, but also include rehabilitation, physical therapy, medical aides, and devices beyond what your underlying health insurance may cover. In the event of a serious accident, these benefits are important to your recovery. A serious accident will most likely exhaust the state minimum coverage of $5,000. For example, if you are involved in an accident that requires you to be transported by helicopter to a trauma center, the cost can easily be $7,500 or more, exhausting your minimum coverage.

If your medical benefits exhaust and you have health insurance coverage, your health insurance becomes the appropriate source of payment for your accident related medical expenses. If you do not have health insurance coverage, you should purchase additional benefits to protect yourself because the insurance carrier of the at-fault party does not have to directly pay your medical expenses until your claim has settled or an award is reached at trial.

It is also worth noting that if you rely upon a Health Maintenance Organization (HMO), an employer sponsored self-funded health care plan, or government plan such as Medicaid, Medicare, or a Medicare Advantage Plan, your health insurer may be entitled to subrogation from your settlement or verdict. The right of subrogation provides that in the event of a successful recovery against a negligent party, the entity providing medical coverage has a right to be reimbursed.

Wage Loss Reimbursement

First-party benefits include optional wage loss reimbursement. There is a five day waiting period to receive wage loss reimbursement. Wage loss reimbursement can be purchased in the amount of $5,000 or greater, or it can be waived. Wage loss reimbursement covers 80% of your wage and may be subject to a monthly maximum such as $1,000. At Berger and Green, we suggest that you do not waive your income loss benefits. Though optional, income loss benefits are very important. If you are injured in an accident, the insurance carrier for the at-fault party will not give consideration or pay your wage loss until the claim has settled or a jury awards you damages. This leaves those employed, but unable to return to work, and who do not have disability coverage through their employer, without any income until they are able to return to work or their claim is settled. If you purchase first party income loss benefits, your insurance carrier will pay monthly payments to you, provided your doctor produces proof of disability and your employer provides proof of employment and income.

Eligibility For First Party Benefits

You are eligible for first party benefits if you have purchased these benefits from your insurer or if you meet certain criteria detailed below. In order to obtain first party benefits, an application for first party coverage has to be completed, signed by you, and submitted to your own automobile insurance carrier. Should you not have automobile insurance but live in a household where there is an active automobile insurance policy, you can obtain first party benefits through the policy of a resident relative. If you do not have your own policy or live in a household with a relative who has an active insurance policy, you have a right to seek first party benefits from the insurer of the vehicle you occupied. If you were a pedestrian, you would have a right to seek first party benefits through the insurance carrier of any vehicle involved in the accident in which you were injured.

Limited Versus Full Tort

In Pennsylvania, purchasers of motor vehicle insurance coverage have the option to purchase a full tort policy or a limited tort policy. If full tort coverage is purchased, a victim of an accident has the right to make a claim for not only lost wages and medical expense reimbursement but also for pain and suffering, no matter what your injuries may be. If limited tort coverage is purchased, the policyholder has a slightly reduced automobile insurance premium but gives up the right to make claims for pain and suffering damages unless they have sustained a serious injury which is defined as death, disfigurement, or the serious impairment of a bodily function.

We strongly encourage you to select a full tort policy. In fact, if you are reading this book we suggest you call your insurance carrier today and make sure that you have selected full tort coverage.

If you choose limited tort and are involved in an accident but do not sustain serious injuries, you will be precluded from recovering pain and suffering damages. There are exceptions to this law, including if the injuries sustained were caused by a driver who pleads guilty or is found guilty of driving under the influence of alcohol or drugs, or if the injuries are caused by an out of state vehicle. You should consult with an attorney to determine if other exceptions may apply.

Pain and Suffering

If you have selected full tort coverage you can make a claim for pain and suffering damages. Pain and suffering damages include physical pain and suffering, emotional distress, loss of life's enjoyment, and disfigurement. These are considered noneconomic detriment, meaning things that you cannot place a dollar amount on. If you have selected limited tort coverage you cannot make a claim for pain and suffering damages unless you sustained a serious injury which is defined by law as death, disfigurement, or the serious impairment of a bodily function. If you select limited tort and sustain an injury with an extensive healing process such as a fractured hip, from which you make a full and complete recovery, you may be unable to make a claim because the accident did not cause death, disfigurement, or the serious impairment of a bodily function. We often see people with serious injuries who have suffered greatly due to an accident caused by another's negligence who cannot be compensated for their pain and suffering because they selected limited tort coverage.

Bodily Injury Liability

In Pennsylvania there is a minimum limit of bodily injury liability that you must carry on your insurance policy. At the time of this publication, the minimum limit is $15,000 per person and $30,000 per accident or occurrence. Bodily Injury or Liability Coverage is the amount of insurance that you purchase to cover injuries and damages which you cause as a result of your own fault or carelessness. We strongly encourage that you purchase a policy limit greater than the state minimum. If you are at fault in a motor vehicle accident that leaves the injured party with serious injuries, your minimum policy limit coverage will not cover the medical expenses or compensate the victim for their total damages. In order to recover their expenses, including medical bills, the injured accident victim may be forced to go after your personal assets. In order to protect your personal assets we suggest a policy with limits of $100,000 per person and $300,000 per accident or occurrence.

If you are a victim in an accident, the bodily injury liability coverage of the at-fault party will determine the amount of damages you can collect from his or her insurance carrier. If you purchase uninsured/underinsured motorist coverage (UM/UIM) you can recover damages from your own insurance carrier.

Uninsured/Underinsured Motorist Benefits Coverage (UM/UIM)

Uninsured and underinsured motorist benefits protect you if you have been injured in an accident and the at-fault party has inadequate or no insurance. You are eligible to obtain the same amount of uninsured and underinsured motorist benefits coverage as your liability coverage (the coverage that applies when you are at fault for an accident and injure someone else). For example, if you purchase the recommended amount of liability insurance of at least $100,000 per person and $300,000 per accident or occurrence, you are eligible for uninsured and underinsured motorist benefits coverage in the same amount. UM/UIM coverage applies to drivers, passengers, and pedestrians injured in motor vehicle accidents. In certain instances where stacking is permitted, you may be able to recover more. Stacking allows the UM/UIM coverage to be increased based on the number of vehicles under which you are an insured.

Specifically, uninsured motorist benefits protects you if you sustain injuries in an accident caused by a driver who has no insurance or a driver who leaves the scene of an accident without identifying himself and who cannot be identified later. If your injury is caused by a driver who leaves the scene of the accident without identifying himself, you must report the accident to the police and to your insurance company as soon as it is practical in order to have a valid claim for uninsured motorist benefits.

Underinsured motorist benefits protect you in the event that an accident is caused by a negligent driver who has insufficient coverage to compensate you for your damages. Once you exhaust the liability coverage of the at-fault driver's insurance policy, you can make a claim to your own insurance carrier for underinsured motorist benefits. In order to accept the at-fault driver's liability insurance and settle your claim, you need written permission from your own insurance carrier.

You may elect to not purchase uninsured and underinsured motorist benefits coverage, or purchase the coverage at a lower amount than your liability insurance. We strongly discourage this as there are many drivers in the Commonwealth of Pennsylvania who fail to purchase auto insurance or who purchase the state minimum coverage. Protect yourself and your family by carrying uninsured and underinsured motorist benefits coverage in the same amount as your liability coverage.

Stacking Your Insurance Coverage

Stacking your underinsured and uninsured motorist benefits will multiply your coverage in the event you or your family members are injured in a motor vehicle accident. Stacking is an option that you can choose when you purchase car insurance. We recommend that if you do not have your underinsured and uninsured motorist benefits stacked that you call your insurance company today to do this. Stacking is based on the number of vehicles in your household. If you have two vehicles and you stack your policy of $100,000 per person and $300,000 per accident or occurrence, you will increase your coverage limit to $200,000 per person and $600,000 per accident or occurrence. Stacking your insurance is an inexpensive way to gain more uninsured and underinsured motorists benefits coverage.

There are two options for stacking your auto insurance coverage. Intra-policy stacking allows you to stack the uninsured and underinsured motorist benefits for each vehicle on the policy. For example, if you have your vehicle, your spouse's vehicle, and your child's vehicle on the same policy, you can stack the UM/UIM benefits for all vehicles.

In Pennsylvania, you can also stack your UM/UIM coverage if you have more than one vehicle and more than one insurance policy within your household.

It is disheartening when we speak with someone that has been injured at the hands of a party with minimum policy limits and the person we are speaking with does not have uninsured and underinsured motorist benefits coverage. You are limited in the damages you can collect if you do not have a policy with uninsured and underinsured motorist benefits. When selecting your insurance policy you must think about the health and well-being of yourself and your family. It only makes sense that you have UM/UIM coverage in the same amount as your liability coverage and that, when possible, you have this coverage stacked. Please take care when signing documents from your insurance carrier that you do not waive these important benefits.

Liability and Property Damage

At the time of this publication, the state minimum liability coverage in Pennsylvania for property damage is $5,000. This amount is to cover the costs of damages you are responsible for in a motor vehicle accident. If you are at fault in a motor vehicle accident, your property damage coverage will pay for the repairs to the accident victim's vehicle. You can also be held responsible for any damage to property that occurs in an accident such as to houses, fences, mailboxes, light posts, and any other damage to a property that you cause. It is important to note that your property damage liability coverage on your insurance policy is not to fix repairs to your vehicle in the event of an accident. The coverage applies only to property damage caused by your actions.

At Berger and Green, we recommend that you purchase property damage coverage in an amount greater than the minimum $5,000. If you cause an accident, you are responsible for the cost to repair all property damage that you cause. Damage to a vehicle or even to multiple vehicles can quickly exceed the minimum policy limit. We recommend that you purchase property coverage at a minimum amount of $25,000 in order to protect your personal assets.

Making A Claim For Property Damage

If you are involved in an accident caused by the carelessness of another, you will go to your source of insurance coverage for payment of medical expenses and lost wages. You also have a choice of making a claim for property damage under your own insurance policy which will pay for your vehicle damage less your deductible or you may make your claim against the other person's insurance carrier. If you rely on your own insurance company, it will pay your property damage and thereafter seek reimbursement of the amount paid to you from the insurance policy of the at fault driver. Additionally, this will include reimbursement of your deductible which will eventually be sent to you.

Collision and Comprehensive Coverage

Collision and Comprehensive Coverage are optional coverages that you can add to your policy. Collision coverage pays for the damages to your vehicle if you are involved in an accident. This could be a single car accident or multi-vehicle accident and is regardless of fault. Comprehensive coverage will cover any damage to your car that is not caused by a motor vehicle accident. Examples of instances covered by comprehensive coverage include theft, weather-related events, and if you hit a deer or other animal. A common use for comprehensive insurance is to pay for a cracked or broken windshield. There is often a deductible associated with collision and comprehensive coverage. Though collision and comprehensive insurance is not required by law in Pennsylvania, it is required by the bank if your vehicle is leased or financed.

You also have the option to contact the at-fault party's insurance company and have them agree to pay for the damages to your vehicle. If the cost of repairing the damage to your vehicle exceeds 80% of its value then the insurance carrier may declare the vehicle a total loss. Upon the surrendering of your title, the insurance carrier will pay the value of your vehicle.

Catastrophic Loss Benefits

Insurers are also required to offer catastrophic loss benefits that provide medical coverage after $100,000 and up to $1,000,000. Catastrophic loss coverage is relatively inexpensive and if a catastrophic event occurred this coverage would cover medically necessary expenses not traditionally covered by your underlying insurances such as a wheelchair accessible van, motorized wheelchair, and accessibility improvements to your home.

Pennsylvania Financial Responsibility Assigned Claims Plan

For Pennsylvania residents there is a source of insurance coverage if you are involved in a motor vehicle accident which is not your fault and for which you have no source of first party benefits. This would be from the Pennsylvania Financial Responsibility Assigned Claims Plan. Unfortunately, the amount of benefits available is only $15,000. This plan does not protect you if you own a registered vehicle that is not insured.

State Law Requires Car Insurance

The Commonwealth of Pennsylvania requires owners of motor vehicles to have financial responsibility, i.e. auto insurance. If your insurance policy lapses you are required by law to mail your license plates to PENNDOT in

Harrisburg, PA. If you fail to do this and you are involved in an accident you are not eligible for first party benefits.

CHAPTER 6

YOUR MEDICAL BILLS

If you have been involved in an accident you are most likely concerned about who will pay your medical bills. In Pennsylvania, the primary source of payment for your medical bills is your own automobile insurance. This coverage is your first party benefits. If you are involved in a motor vehicle accident, even if it is your own fault, you have a right to first party benefits which include reimbursement of your medical expenses. The amount of coverage for medical expenses is dependent on the amount you purchased. We strongly encourage that you purchase more than the state minimum amount of $5,000. If you do not own a vehicle and or do not have automobile insurance, the second source of medical benefits would be through the automobile insurance carrier of a relative with whom you reside. If you do not have automobile insurance and do not reside with a relative who has auto insurance, you may make a claim for medical coverage through the vehicle that you occupied, or if you were a pedestrian through the insurance carrier of any vehicle involved in the accident.

It does not matter if you were a victim of a car accident or the negligent party, first-party benefits will cover the costs of your medical expenses. For this reason, we strongly encourage that you have more than the minimum state limit of first-party benefits. Your own insurance policy will first cover your medical expenses. If you do not have an insurance policy, your medical care will be covered by the insurance policy of a relative with whom you reside. If you do not meet either of these circumstances you will apply for medical care from the insurance policy of the owner of the vehicle you were in when the accident occurred.

Medical Expenses Exceed First Party Benefits

When purchasing auto insurance you choose a maximum limit for medical benefits coverage. If you are in an accident and your medical bills exceed your first party benefits, the secondary source of medical coverage is your own health insurance policy. Your health insurance may be a private plan or a government plan. Your automobile insurance carrier will inform you when your first party benefits have been exhausted. At this time, the remaining bills should be submitted to your health insurance provider for payment. It is important to note that some health care coverage contains provisions that require you to reimburse them if you are successful in obtaining money damages from the at fault driver.

Medicare

If your health insurance plan is Medicare, your medical bills will be paid by Medicare once your first party benefits have been exhausted. You must have a Medicare health insurance policy for Medicare to pay your medical bills. Please be advised that your government provided health care plan may have a right of subrogation, which means that in the event of a successful recovery against a negligent party, the entity providing medical coverage has a right to be reimbursed.

Medicaid

If you receive Medicaid, your medical bills will be paid through the Department of Human Services once your first party benefits have been exhausted. You must have a Medicaid health insurance policy for Medicaid to pay your medical bills. Please be advised that your government provided health care plan may have a right of subrogation, which means that in the event of a successful recovery against a negligent party the entity providing medical coverage has a right to be reimbursed

Reimbursement Of Your Medical Expenses

The insurance carrier of the at-fault party is responsible to pay for and or reimburse you for medical expenses not covered by insurance, deductibles, co-pays, and eligible subrogation claims asserted by health insurance carriers up to the applicable limit of liability insurance at statutorily defined reimbursement rates. These expenses become part of your general damage claim, which includes out of pocket expenses in addition to compensation for pain and suffering. This is all subject to available coverage. It is important to note that all damages, including out of pocket medical expenses, are paid at the end of the case once you sign a release and not during the pendency of the claim.

How Your Attorney Can Help With Your Medical Bills

At Berger and Green we assist our clients in securing their first party benefits, assist with medical expense reimbursement, and wage loss reimbursement. Additionally, we monitor your insurance carrier to determine that the appropriate amount of money is paid for medical expense reimbursement and for wage loss reimbursement. We do not charge for this service. Medical expense reimbursement for accident related injuries in motor vehicle cases is made under the terms of the applicable automobile insurance policy providing coverage. It is done in accordance with the terms of the policy and the level of those benefits purchased. To put it simply, we will help you navigate through this difficult task of determining if your medical bills are being paid appropriately and we will keep track of your out of pocket expenses so that these can be added to your claim for damages.

CHAPTER 7
THE VALUE OF YOUR CASE

If you are reading this book, chances are you or someone you love has been injured in an accident and you want to make sure that you recover as much in damages as you are allowed by law to compensate for your injuries. We understand this. It is our mission to obtain for our clients the highest possible settlement or result consistent with the facts and circumstances of the accident and the nature of the injuries inflicted upon them as well as any permanent conditions that ensue. It is not appropriate or responsible to attempt to list a figure on a claim shortly after an accident has happened and without being able to determine the full range of injuries and damages sustained by the client.

Factors That Influence Value

The value of your case is dependent upon the facts and circumstances of how the accident happened, the injuries that you suffered, the length of time that you are under medical management, whether or not you have any permanent or ongoing problems, what your treating physicians say about your condition and its consequences, and the county in which you may file suit. There are other factors which provide value in a claim, such as whether the accident was caused by a driver under the influence of alcohol or drugs, or whether the at-fault driver acted in a manner that showed a reckless disregard for human life. Additionally, we take into consideration whether there are any obligations to pay outstanding medical expenses or reimburse medical expenses that have been paid. The loss of income and future earning potential also impacts the value of the case. These damages vary by the age of the injured party and their level of education.

Items that must be taken into consideration include the length of time you are under treatment, what your doctor says about your recovery, any disability or limitations, and any ongoing problems you may have. Other factors include the strength of your liability case, whether you were also at fault, and the venue in which a lawsuit would be filed.

The appropriate time to determine the value of a case is after evaluating medical records. We need to determine what the treating physicians say about the healing process and any ongoing problems, review physical therapy records and surgery operative reports, evaluate whether there is scarring or deformities, and consult with a treating specialist. Once the evidence has been collected, we are then in a position to evaluate the aspects of the claim which include unpaid medical expenses and future medical expenses, unpaid wages and any future wages, loss of earning capacity, out of pocket expenses and the pain and suffering portion of any claim. If you are married, your spouse may also have a claim for a loss of consortium, which is the help, companionship, and marital relations of your spouse. In cases of catastrophic injuries we also consider the cost of long term care (nursing home or in-home care), the consequences of loss of limbs, paralysis, or the death of our client and the claim for wrongful death and survival benefits brought by the personal representative of the estate of the victim against those responsible. It is our job to build a strong claim for damages for you. We will outline ways that we do this in the subsequent sections.

In a perfect world an injured party should be able to seek and obtain fair, reasonable, and adequate compensation from an insurance carrier representing a careless individual that causes an accident. Unfortunately, we do not live in a perfect world and the only way an injured party can avoid being taken advantage of is to hire competent counsel.

Determining Value When There Is A Catastrophic Injury or Death

Catastrophic injuries are life altering and require consideration of the needs of the injured party including future care, medical treatment, rehabilitation, skilled nursing care, reconfiguration of living arrangements, and mobility aides over the course of the injured party's natural life.

Unfortunately there is often inadequate insurance coverage. This is why we sometimes recommend consideration of a special needs trust so that the injured party's recovery is segregated and used for special purposes and still allow the injured party to receive benefits provided by the government.

In the devastating event of a fatality, the conscious pain and suffering of the victim and their earnings over the balance of their work life are factors when determining the value of the case.

The spouse of an injured accident victim has their own derivative claim for loss of consortium. This loss encompasses the denial of the service of his or her spouse, the spouse's aide, and comfort. Loss of consortium claims have even more importance in claims where there is a catastrophic injury or death.

CHAPTER 8

BUILDING YOUR CASE

At Berger and Green, all of our cases are thoroughly investigated and prepared to determine all responsible parties and the extent of our client's injuries and damages. Your attorney is responsible for finding all potential sources of insurance coverage that are available. We begin investigating and building your case from the moment you become our client.

Medical Evidence

Medical evidence is key to a successful personal injury claim. The gathering of medical evidence starts with obtaining EMS trip reports and includes every hospital stay, doctor visit, therapy session, medication, surgery, and any other treatment you receive. Your attorney will also request itemized statements from every provider. Expert medical reports may be requested from key treatment providers.

Keep A Calendar

It is important that you keep a calendar of all medically-related events. This includes doctor visits, medical testing, and physical therapy sessions. Please make note of what your physician states at each appointment. It is important that you share with your physician how you are feeling. For example, if you are in a lot of pain or are suffering from anxiety related to the accident, let your doctor know. These symptoms should be entered into your medical records.

Keep A Diary

We ask our clients to keep a diary of how they are feeling both physically and emotionally as they recover from their accident to share with us. This is especially true when a person suffers a serious injury where the recovery time can span multiple months or even years. There may be a time during your case where you will be asked to describe your injuries, your limitations, and your pain. This diary will serve as documentation of your pain and suffering.

Photograph Your Injuries

Photographs of your injuries will be used in the demand we send to the insurance company and will speak volumes at a trial if necessary. We ask that you take pictures at every stage of the healing process. Document your injuries with photographs while in the hospital, following a procedure, and at home. This would include photographs of bruising, scarring, lacerations, and any necessary medical device used for the healing process.

Evaluating Medical Records

The attorneys at Berger and Green evaluate medical records every day. This experience is critical when compiling the evidence that supports your claim for damages. When reviewing your medical records, we are looking at the time you spent in the hospital, your procedures, how long you were treated by your physicians, and your medications. We want to see that, if necessary, you are being seen by a specialist. For example, if you have a broken arm we want to see that you have been treated by an orthopedist. Your medical records play a large part in determining the value of your claim.

The insurance company will not take your word or that of your attorney in their evaluation of your claim. Your injuries must be documented in your medical records. This is why seeing a specialist, having testing such as an MRI, and going to physical therapy support your claim that you have sustained a serious injury.

Police Reports

If you have been injured in a motor vehicle accident, one of the first steps we will take as your representative is to request the appropriate police report. This report lists relevant information such as the insurance carrier for the vehicles, the drivers, owners, and occupants of the vehicles, and witnesses to the accident.

The Accident Scene

We obtain photographs of the accident scene as well as photographs of the damage to the vehicles or the defective condition that contributed to the accident. This might include overgrown bushes that obstruct an intersection which contributed to the cause of an accident or any dangerous road condition. We ask that you preserve any evidence that you may have in your possession. For example, if you took photographs on your phone of the accident scene, we ask that you forward them to us and do not delete them.

Witnesses

When necessary we contact witnesses to determine what they saw and what they know about the event. A witness to the case may be a bystander or another occupant of the vehicle in which you were traveling. It is important to obtain the contact information of any witnesses before they leave the scene.

Accident Reconstruction

In appropriate circumstances, we retain an accident reconstruction specialist to render an opinion regarding exactly how the accident occurred, what speed the vehicles were traveling, and an opinion as to the fault of the person. While this is not necessary for every case to reach a settlement, in instances where we are forced to go to trial, the testimony of the accident reconstruction specialist can paint a picture of the accident scene for the jurors.

Experts

Experts are used in a personal injury case in instances where their opinion can be used to establish liability, causation, and or damages. For instance, a doctor who is treating your injuries may express an opinion as to the cause of your injury, your prognosis, and future medical expenses. We will obtain an engineer when there are contributing factors to the cause of the accident such as defectively designed intersections, failure to have proper signage on roadways, and whether certain products were defectively designed.

CHAPTER 9

NEGOTIATIONS WITH THE INSURANCE COMPANY

A detailed demand letter along with supporting documentation is sent to the insurance company of the at-fault party. Supporting documentation includes the police report and the investigative materials, photographs, medical documentation including hospital records and physician's office notes, itemized statements, and reports from any physicians. Within the demand, we outline the facts of the accident, our theory of liability, and a demand for money damages on behalf of our clients. A demand letter is sent when our client has reached maximum medical improvement. Examples of maximum medical improvement can be when your physician has released you from treatment or if your condition is not expected to improve or worsen.

The Timing Of The Demand

The statute of limitations in an automobile accident case is two years from the date of the accident for adults in Pennsylvania. The statute of limitations in an automobile accident for minors under the age of eighteen is two years after their eighteenth birthday. A demand should not be sent too early in the case as we want to make sure that your physicians are able to provide an accurate future prognosis. It is also important that the demand is sent with enough time for the insurance company to properly review and request additional information, if necessary.

Damages Included Within the Demand

Damages are made up of both economic and noneconomic detriment. Economic detriment has a monetary value that is easily determined. Noneconomic detriment has a monetary value that is subject to interpretation. Both forms of damages are taken into consideration when determining the value of your case.

In Pennsylvania, your tort option plays a part in the type of damages you are entitled to recover. If you have selected limited tort coverage, you cannot make a claim for pain and suffering damages unless you have sustained a serious injury which is defined by law as death, disfigurement, or the serious impairment of a bodily function.

Noneconomic damages consist of pain and suffering, loss of life's pleasures, emotional distress, and loss of consortium. The monetary value of noneconomic damages is subjective. It is the job of your attorney to explain the significance of these losses.

Some examples of economic damages are unreimbursed medical expenses, future medical expenses, lost wages, and lost earning capacity. At Berger and Green, we keep a record of any monetary expenses that are outstanding or have been paid out of your pocket, so that you can be compensated upon resolution of your case.

In the instance of lost earning capacity, we consult with a vocational expert or economist to project your earnings through your retirement age. This expert would author a report which is used to show what you would have made throughout your life at your employment prior to being injured in an accident.

We can also consult with a life-care planner to project your medical expenses or medical accommodations needed over the course of your natural life. The value determined by the life-care planner is taken into consideration by the at-fault party's insurance company during its evaluation of the claim.

We understand that being injured in an accident can be a painful and emotional time in your life. At Berger and Green, we want to make sure that you are fully compensated for the monetary and nonmonetary detriments that make this time difficult.

An Offer From The Insurance Company

We have an extensive conversation with the insurance company to explain in detail how the accident has affected your life and why we are seeking damages in the amount that has been demanded on your behalf. In response, the insurance carrier sets forth an initial offer of settlement which we will convey to you. We will discuss the offer and make a recommendation about whether we feel this is a fair, reasonable, and adequate settlement or whether we recommend that you not accept the offer and allow us to go back and seek more. This is a negotiation process that goes back and forth until the insurance company makes what it says is its highest, best, and final offer. At that point, we assess the final offer and make a recommendation to you about whether we feel this to be a fair, reasonable and adequate offer or whether we feel it to be inadequate. In the latter case, we may recommend that a lawsuit be filed.

Accepting The Offer

The decision to accept an offer of settlement always belongs with the client. It is your claim and you have the final decision, even if that means accepting an offer that we feel should be rejected. Often clients just want to get the claim over with and do not want the stress and time involved in proceeding through trial. In considering whether to accept an offer of settlement, we determine whether there are any existing liens from private healthcare providers, Medicare, the Pennsylvania Department of Human Services, or treating medical providers. If there are liens on your settlement funds, we try to negotiate those liens so that we can maximize the extent of your recovery. In the event that the final settlement offer is in our determination inadequate, and our client authorizes us to file a lawsuit on his or her behalf, we do so in the county in which the accident occurred or where the responsible party resides. The general rule in Pennsylvania is that the suit must be brought within two years of the date of the accident in matters involving injuries to adults. In matters involving injuries to a minor under the age of 18 years old, a suit must be commenced no later than the minor's 20th birthday.

Arbitration

Arbitration is when both parties agree to submit the claim to a neutral party for determination as to fault and value. There is no appeal from the neutral party's decision unless there is a showing of fraud. This is a faster and less expensive way to resolve a case than through a trial in the Court of Common Pleas.

Mediation

Mediation is when both parties appear before a neutral mediator who attempts to reach a consensus between the injured party and the at-fault party regarding the disposition of the case. Mediation can be binding or non-binding. If it is binding, the mediator determines the value of the case. If an agreement is not reached in a non-binding mediation, the parties will continue litigation in the Court of Common Pleas.

CHAPTER 10

FILING A LAW SUIT

The decision to file a law suit is made when a settlement is not reached with the insurance company prior to the expiration of the statute of limitations. We understand that this can be an intimidating step in moving forward with your claim. At Berger and Green we have lawyers who are experienced in litigating personal injury cases.

Suit may be commenced by the filing of a Praecipe for Writ of Summons with the Prothonotary of the county in which the event occurred or where the Defendant(s) resides. That Writ of Summons is delivered to the Sheriff for service on the Defendant(s).

The matter may also be commenced by the filing of a Complaint in Civil Action with the office of the Prothonotary. The Complaint is delivered to the Sheriff for service on the Defendant(s).

The Complaint in Civil Action sets forth the names of the parties, factual allegations, who is responsible, the acts of carelessness or negligence, and the damages inflicted. The Complaint in Civil Action commences the lawsuit and it then enters the discovery phase.

The Discovery Phase

In the discovery phase, attorneys for the Plaintiff and Defendant exchange Interrogatories, which are written questions to be answered, as well as a Request for Production of Documents. The discovery phase is the exchanging of evidence and information between all parties. Depositions of the parties, witnesses, doctors, and experts who will be testifying at trial are scheduled. Depositions are a form of testimony where the attorneys for each party have the opportunity to ask the opposing party questions related to the case. The deposition is recorded by a court reporter.

During the discovery phase, it is likely that the defense will request that you be seen by a physician of its choosing.

Reaching A Settlement During Litigation

Many cases settle after discovery is commenced and before trial. Your attorney will take every opportunity to explore settlement at appropriate times. The discovery process allows the insurance carrier of the at-fault party and its attorneys to assess the at-fault party's negligence and the extent of the plaintiff's injuries and damages.

Pre-Trial

The Pre-Trial Statement outlines the case, including your damages, witnesses, and exhibits. A Pre-Trial Conference is held with the judge assigned to the case in an attempt to narrow the issues and determine whether the case can be resolved prior to trial. Prior to the trial itself, your attorney will have in-depth meetings to prepare you so that you feel comfortable in understanding what will occur at the trial. It is important that you understand your role and what questions you will be asked. Your attorney will meet and prepare witnesses, coordinate with experts, and prepare exhibits that are presented at time of trial.

Jury Selection

Jurors are selected by the attorneys for both parties. Your attorney and the defense attorney will have an opportunity to submit questions to be asked of the jurors. Your attorney will then have a limited opportunity to remove jurors whom he or she feels are biased or who he or she thinks would be unfavorable to your case. Jury selection is one of the most important aspects of your case. The litigation attorneys at Berger and Green have experience in selecting jurors.

The Trial

The trial starts with an opening statement from your attorney. The opening statement is not testimony or evidence, but rather an explanation of the case, what will be proven, and the role of the jury. The defense also has an opportunity to make an opening statement. The case is then presented through the testimony of the Plaintiff as well as the Plaintiff's witnesses, experts, and exhibits. The Defendant has an opportunity to cross examine the Plaintiff and then present its case. The Plaintiff's attorney then has an opportunity to cross examine the Defendant.

Closing Statement

Each side has an opportunity to make a closing statement. This is a summary of the trial and a final appeal to the jurors. The judge then instructs the jurors on the law.

Jury Instructions

At the conclusion of the trial, the judge will instruct the jury on the law, the manner of deliberations, and the completion of the verdict form. Before the judge instructs the jury, the attorneys are given an opportunity to suggest which instructions should be given. For this reason, it is important to have an attorney who is knowledgeable of the law applicable to a personal injury case.

Verdict

If there is no appeal taken from the jury verdict, the insurance carrier for the Defendant issues a check in the amount of the jury verdict made payable to the law firm and the Plaintiff.

The attorney thereafter disburses funds in accordance with the retainer agreement and makes reimbursement to any lienholders.

PART TWO

CHAPTER 11

TRUCK ACCIDENT INJURIES

When someone has been involved in an accident involving a tractor-trailer or a large truck, the aftermath can be devastating. Because of the size and weight of these vehicles, victims suffer serious and sometimes fatal injuries.

The average automobile weighs about 5,000 pounds. In comparison, loaded commercial semi-trucks can weigh up to 80,000 pounds. In some cases, the truck may be carrying freight that is highly flammable or hazardous. When a commercial truck is on the road, it is important for other drivers to be aware of the truck's limitations and its blind spots.

Careless driving on behalf of the truck driver can cause serious accidents. This can be due to inadequate training or a schedule that requires the driver to travel long distances for extended periods of time. Truck drivers work long and exhausting shifts. However, it is still their responsibility to practice safe driving at all times. Sadly, this is not always the case.

According to federal law, truck drivers are to work a maximum of 14 hours a shift and may only work the maximum after ten consecutive hours off duty.

In addition to driver error and fatigue, there are many causes of truck accidents including overloading of the truck, unsecured or improperly loaded cargo, a failure to maintain the vehicle to all safety standards, failure of the driver or company to follow safety regulations, or a mechanical defect of the truck.

Following an accident, the truck's driver will most often be represented by his or her employer and the insurer of the vehicle. These are often large companies or corporations who have legal departments and attorneys who handle all matters related to an accident involving their employees. Do not hesitate to contact an experienced personal injury attorney if you are injured in an accident involving a truck. The driver of the truck will not hesitate to have an attorney working on his or her side.

Chapter 12

Motorcycle Accident Injuries

Motorcycle accidents generally fall into two categories: a one-vehicle crash or a two or more vehicle crash. A one-vehicle crash involves a motorcyclist crashing or hitting an object such as a light post or guard rail. It would also include a crash due to a defect in the motorcycle itself. A two or more vehicle crash is when a motorcycle is involved in an accident with one or more other vehicles.

Regardless of the type of motorcycle accident, the injuries sustained in these crashes can be life threatening. Two of the most common types of injuries sustained are broken bones and head injuries.

Broken bones are common injuries sustained in motorcycle accidents due to the motorcyclist's lack of protection. Unlike an occupant of a vehicle, the motorcyclist does not have the same protection when struck by a vehicle. They are struck directly and are often thrown from the motorcycle itself. Broken bones can debilitate a person from working and doing every day functions.

Head injuries can include traumatic brain injuries, concussions, seizures, paralysis, and more. These types of injuries can range from mild to severe and may result in permanent disability or even death. No matter the severity, head injuries should never be taken lightly.

Motorcycle Helmet Laws

Although helmet laws vary by state, motorcyclists should consider the risks of an injury if an accident were to occur. Helmets are proven to reduce the risk of head injuries and death.

In Pennsylvania, a helmet is not required by law for drivers who are over the age of 21 and have either had their motorcycle license for at least two full years or have completed a motorcycle rider safety course. The motorcycle rider safety course must be approved by the state or the Motorcycle Safety Foundation.

In Ohio, a helmet is required for all drivers under the age of 18 and all new or novice drivers. Ohio issues novice licenses to new motorcycle operators over the age of 18 who have never held a motorcycle license in Ohio or other recognized states.

In West Virginia, all motorcycle drivers are required to wear a helmet.

It is important to know the helmet laws in your state and surrounding states in the event that you are involved in a motorcycle accident. Your state's helmet law may play a large role in whether you can recover compensation for any resulting neck or head injuries.

Passengers on motorcycles rely on drivers to get them to their destinations safely. As a passenger you have no control over the motorcycle yet may still bear the devastating aftermath if involved in an accident. If you are a passenger who has been involved in a motorcycle accident, you can recover personal injury damages against the motorcycle operator and any other driver who caused the accident.

A motorcycle accident is terrifying for all parties involved. There are certain things you can do after an accident to help support a potential personal injury claim. Following a motorcycle accident, it is important to get the contact information of everyone involved in the accident and anyone who witnessed the accident. The police should be notified so that that the accident can be officially recorded. If possible insist that all drivers and witness stay until the police arrive. If the crash occurred due to a defect in your motorcycle, do not have the bike repaired until you are able to contact an attorney.

If you have been involved in a motorcycle accident, you may be able to file a personal injury claim for injuries sustained or a product liability claim if there was a mechanical defect in your motorcycle to help compensate you for medical bills, lost wages, and pain and suffering.

It is understandable that you may sustain injuries too severe to be able to follow these recommendations. If this is the case, try to ask a witness or relative to help the best he or she can. The most important thing for individuals who have been involved in a motorcycle accident to do is to seek the medical treatment they need.

CHAPTER 13
WRONGFUL DEATH

The loss of a loved one due to another's negligence can have devastating consequences for a family. A wrongful death claim may be filed when someone is involved in an accident that results in death.

A wrongful death claim can be pursued against a negligent party who has caused an injury resulting in death. Examples of a negligent party in a wrongful death claim include the at-fault driver in a motor vehicle accident, the person responsible for constructing a faulty roadway, a manufacturer of a defective vehicle, and a person (or establishment) who sold and served alcohol to a visibly impaired individual.

Damages In A Wrongful Death and Survival Claim

In a wrongful death claim, the spouse, children, or parents of the deceased may bring a claim to recover damages sustained as a result of their loved one's death. There are many factors involved in determining the recoverable damages in a wrongful death claim. Medical expenses, funeral expenses, burial expenses, and estate administration expenses are damages that can be quantified. Other compensation may not be so easily determined. This includes an amount of compensation that will fairly and adequately compensate the family of the decedent (i.e. wife, children, parents) for the loss of any contributions they would have received between the time of the death of the decedent and today. This could include food, clothing, shelter, medical care, and education. In addition, a claim may be made for compensation to the spouse and children for loss of services the decedent would have provided, such as guidance or moral upbringing. Due to the complexity of determining the damages the decedent's family may recover, it is advisable that you contact an experienced personal injury attorney.

Wrongful death actions involve a thorough investigation into the facts of the case. It is necessary to gather all documentation, consult with forensic economists and medical experts, negotiate with insurance companies, and when necessary prepare for trial. Your attorney will seek to recover projected lost earnings, pain and suffering, medical bills and funeral expenses. It is best to consult with a qualified and experienced wrongful death attorney as soon as possible following the tragic loss of a loved one. The attorneys at Berger and Green can help you through this difficult and complex period. While we understand that no amount of money can truly compensate you for your loss, our attorneys will fight to obtain the compensation you deserve.

CHAPTER 14

DOG BITE INJURIES

According to the American Humane Association, there are an estimated 4.7 million dog bite incidents in the United States each year. Of that number, 50% involve children under 12 years old.

The reason that young children are more susceptible to these injuries may be their age. Children might not interpret signs that suggest a dog is frightened or aggressive that an adult may recognize more quickly.

A significant number of dog bites involve a family dog or a dog with which the victim is familiar. These claims may be covered by insurance. Even in instances where the dog is known, victims should not hesitate to take legal action. Dog bites can cause severe injuries that will affect an individual physically and emotionally for the rest of his or her life.

What To Do Following A Dog Bite

The most important thing to do immediately following a dog bite is to seek appropriate medical attention. If you are able, it is also important to be sure that you can identify the dog involved in the attack and the dog's owner. Gather the contact information of the dog's owner and if possible get the homeowner's insurance and dog license information. If there are any witnesses to the dog attack, get their names, addresses, and telephone numbers. When it is possible, take photos of all injuries sustained in the attack.

If a dog has bitten you or a loved one, it is important to contact a personal injury attorney to discuss your legal rights. Dog bites can cause serious injuries like disfigurement and scarring. These attacks can also be emotionally traumatizing for an individual, especially a young child. At Berger and Green, our attorneys take into account how this incident affects your present and future needs.

CHAPTER 15

PREMISES LIABILITY INJURIES

Slip and falls are typically unexpected and hard to avoid. Because a fall is unexpected, the injuries can be serious. These types of accidents can occur when a property is poorly designed, constructed, or maintained. You may have a personal injury claim if you have sustained injuries in a slip and fall accident.

The attorneys at Berger and Green have helped numerous individuals who have been involved in slip and fall accidents caused by negligent property owners. While a person does have a general responsibility to be aware of his or her surroundings, if you are injured on someone else's property because of a hazard that the owner should have been aware of, or was aware of and ignored, you may have a right to compensation for your injuries. Do not immediately assume the blame for your slip and fall accident.

Common Causes

You may have a claim for compensation for your injuries if you have suffered a slip and fall accident on a residential or commercial property. There are many causes to slip and fall accidents. Common causes of accidents on sidewalks or in parking lots include a defect in the walking surface, a significant drop off or elevation (uneven slabs), a poorly lit walking area, and ice formed by poor drainage conditions. Weather can play a role in slip and fall accidents. If ice and snow that was not cleared within a reasonable period of time after it had stopped accumulating caused your injuries, you should speak with a personal injury attorney. At Berger and Green we also handle cases involving serious falls. This includes stairway falls, balcony falls, and falls that occur at the workplace.

Slip and fall accidents can result in extremely serious injuries to victims. Brain injuries, broken bones, neck and back injuries, and death are all possible. Property owners have the responsibility to ensure that their property is structurally sound and presents no danger to people. Slip and fall claims require great attention to detail, research, and investigation. The attorneys at Berger and Green have the necessary experience and drive to pursue these types of claims to get our clients compensation for the injuries they have sustained.

CHAPTER 16

WORKERS' COMPENSATION

You may not know where to turn if you were injured on the job. Medical bills, wage loss, and future employment are a concern of many. The benefits that you may receive from your employer's insurance carrier will vary depending on the nature and severity of your injuries.

Generally, you may be entitled to payment of your medical bills, wage-loss benefits, temporary or partial disability during the time that you cannot work, and permanent partial disability. If your injuries are severe enough to prohibit you from ever working again, you may be eligible for permanent total disability benefits.

Contacting a workers' compensation attorney will help you understand what your rights are following a work-place accident.

A work-place accident may include cases of exposure to dangerous chemicals, slips and falls, industrial or construction accidents, and accidents that occur while you are traveling for work-related purposes.

An employer may be quick to deny your claim for workers' compensation benefits to protect itself.

Contact A Workers' Compensation Lawyer

You should contact an attorney if: your injuries are severe and require surgery; you and your doctor believe your health will not be the same as it was prior to the injury; you feel that you are unable to go back to work but your employer says that you must return; you want to dispute a decision made by your employer or its insurance company regarding your workers' compensation claim; you feel the benefits that you are receiving are inadequate; your medical benefits have been denied; or you simply do not understand the process and need guidance.

Workers' compensation attorneys usually offer free no obligation consultations and will represent you on a contingent-fee basis. It is important to know that you have options following a work-place accident and that you shouldn't be held responsible for your injuries.

Chapter 17

Product Liability Injuries

When someone is injured while using a product the way that it was intended, the manufacturer of the product as well as the store that sold it may be held liable for injuries. Manufacturers are responsible for making safe products for consumers. The manufacturer and any stores that carry the product must warn consumers of all risks that can occur from using the product. A variety of products can be included in these types of cases, including food, medicines, toys, furniture, household or industrial equipment, and automobiles.

Defective vehicles can cause serious and sometimes fatal injuries. These vehicles are not only a danger to the occupants of the vehicle but also to others on the road. A defect in a vehicle can include faulty brakes, air bags, seat belts, or even the overall design of the vehicle. For example, a vehicle's design may enable it to rollover easily.

People injured by a defective product may be entitled to compensation for their injuries if they were using the product correctly and were seriously hurt as a result.

Product liability cases fall into three categories: (i) the product was not designed properly; (ii) the product was manufactured incorrectly resulting in a defect; and (iii) instructions included with the product were insufficient and did not warn consumers of possible defects.

Building Your Claim

If you were injured while using a product correctly and safely, you may be able to pursue a product liability claim. You will need to gather evidence to support your claim. Save the product along with your receipt for purchase and any manuals or instructions that came with it. Write down when and where you purchased the product. Take photos of the product, the scene of the accident, and any injuries sustained. Gather the contact information of anyone who witnessed your injury.

You have the right to obtain legal advice if you have been injured by a product. It is important to consult an experienced product liability attorney to investigate your case. Companies are quick to place fault on the injured party to protect themselves. Hiring an attorney will help make sure all at-fault parties are held accountable for their negligence.

PART THREE

CHAPTER 18

FREQUENTLY ASKED QUESTIONS

How much does it cost to hire a car accident attorney?

It costs nothing to hire a car accident attorney to represent you in an accident case. Berger and Green attorneys work on a contingent fee basis. This means we will never charge you a fee unless we are able to make a recovery on your behalf. If we are successful, our firm is paid a percentage of what your recovery is and any costs advanced by our firm. When Berger and Green accepts your case, we believe we would be successful at representing you and ultimately getting you compensation for the injuries you sustained.

What if I felt fine after a car accident but notice an injury later?

Many people feel fine and do not bother seeking medical treatment after an accident. Then days later they feel pain they had not felt before. In any case, it is extremely important to seek medical treatment following an accident. Something serious could be wrong and you may not be aware. If you delay getting treatment for too long, your case will be harder to prove. It is very important that you determine whether or not you sustained injuries in a motor vehicle accident. That is why it is important to seek medical attention following an accident. Make sure you clearly tell all medical providers about the accident you were involved in.

Will my auto insurance or health insurance pay my medical cost?

When you have been involved in an accident, you may be wondering who will pay for your medical treatment. If you have both auto insurance and medical insurance, it is important to know where to turn first. Once a claim is opened, your auto insurance will pay for your medical expenses until you have reached the limit of medical coverage you purchased. The amount of coverage will depend on an individual's specific policy. In Pennsylvania, you must have at least $5,000.00 in medical coverage. If your treatment exceeds the limit you purchased, your health insurance will begin to pay for your medical bills.

If I was a passenger in a car whose driver caused a crash, do I have a claim?

When you are the passenger in a car whose driver caused the accident, you may not know where to turn. It is important to know you have options. If you were injured in the accident, you have the right to file a claim against any party that was at fault, even if it is the driver of the vehicle you were in.

If I File a Lawsuit, Will I Have to Testify in Court?

When someone is injured in an accident, whether it be an automobile, slip and fall, or a dog bite, you may have the option to file a claim with an insurance company for the injuries you sustained. When you file a claim, you are submitting medical evidence to the negligent party's insurance company. This involves negotiating until a settlement is reached and all parties have agreed it is adequate. If you hire an attorney, they will be handling the negotiating process for you.

Sometimes an agreement cannot be reached and a lawsuit is filed. Once a lawsuit is filed, it enters the discovery phase where your attorney gathers documentation to prove your case. During this time, the insurance companies can continue to make you additional offers to try and reach a settlement instead of heading to court. If a settlement is not reached before the court date, you may have to go to court to receive compensation for your injuries. If you hire the attorneys at Berger and Green, we will help you every step of the way. We work with you before trial to prepare you for what to expect. This can make testifying in trial easier than you expect.

Why Should I Keep a Calendar in an Injury Claim?

It is important if you are involved in an accident to maintain a calendar that keeps a list of events following the accident and a description of how those events have affected you. Keep track of all of the doctors and medical providers that you have seen so that your attorney can secure medical records from your providers. Also write down how this accident has affected you, the things you cannot do, and the people that have had to assist you. This helps your attorney to document everything that you have gone through. This documentation is helpful if you have to file a law suit. If you have to testify in court, you can refer to your calendar to refresh your memory of the events you have gone through as a result of the accident.

PART FOUR

Chapter 19

Glossary Of Terms

Bodily Injury Liability Coverage – Coverage to be used if you are at fault in an accident and another party is injured. In Pennsylvania, the minimum amount of bodily injury liability coverage you must carry is $15,000 per person and $30,000 per accident.

Collison Coverage – This coverage pays for damage to your vehicle if you are involved in an accident, regardless of fault. In Pennsylvania, this coverage is required if your vehicle is being leased or financed through a bank.

Comprehensive Coverage – This coverage pays for the damage to your vehicle not caused by an automobile accident. In Pennsylvania, this coverage is required if your vehicle is being leased or financed through a bank.

Contingent Fee – A fee that is payable to your attorney upon a favorable out-of-court settlement or jury verdict.

Defendant – The party in which an action is brought against and whom the plaintiff is requesting damages from.

Economic loss – A detriment that has a monetary value.

First party income loss benefits – The benefits provided by a motor vehicle insurance policy to pay for lost wages if you are not able to go to work after an accident. These are typically subject to a five day wait period and a cap of a set amount or 80% of wages.

First party medical benefits – The benefits provided by a motor vehicle insurance policy to pay for the medical treatment and lost wages associated with your accident related injuries.

Full tort – An election made on your policy which allows you to seek compensation for both economic and noneconomic losses suffered as a consequence of the fault of another person regardless of whether or not you sustain a serious injury.

Insured – A party named on an insurance policy or resident relative of a party named on an insurance policy that is providing motor vehicle coverage.

Insurer – An insurance company providing liability coverage.

Limited tort – An election made on your policy that allows you to seek compensation for economic loss only unless you sustain a serious injury.

Loss of Consortium – The loss of society, companionship, and marital relationship which is typically brought by the spouse of an injured party.

Noneconomic loss – A detriment that has a subjective monetary value.

Pain and suffering – The noneconomic damage for the pain and suffering you have endured. Sometimes this term is used to include emotional distress, the loss of life's pleasures, and/or the loss of consortium.

Plaintiff – The party who initiates a civil action. The injured party.

Serious injury – A personal injury resulting in death, permanent disfigurement, or the serious impairment of a bodily function.

Statute of limitations – An established time restriction that limits the amount of time you have to settle a case or file a lawsuit. In Pennsylvania, if you are an adult over the age of 18 in a motor vehicle accident, your statute of limitations is two years from the date of accident. If you are a minor, your statute of limitations is until your 20th birthday. Out of caution, you should treat the expiration date as the day before the two year anniversary or the day before your 20th birthday.

Subrogation – The right of an insurer to pursue reimbursement of payments made by a third party that caused an accident. An example would be a health insurance company recovering an amount paid for medical expenses from the settlement obtained through the motor vehicle insurance coverage.

Underinsured motorist benefits – Coverage that provides protection for a party that has sustained injuries by the owner or operator of a vehicle that does not have sufficient coverage to compensate for damages. This form of coverage is optional and can be rejected.

Uninsured motorist benefits – Coverage that provides protection for a party that has sustained injuries by the owner or operator of a vehicle that is uninsured. This form of coverage is optional and can be rejected.

Stacking – An option you can purchase on your motor vehicle insurance policy which multiplies your uninsured and underinsured coverage by the number of vehicles on your policy, and/or other applicable vehicles.

Made in the USA
Monee, IL
26 September 2021

78836444R00049